SERGE MONAST

THE GREATEST HOAX

NASA'S PROJECT BLUE BEAM

SERGE MONAST

THE GREATEST HOAX

NASA'S PROJECT BLUE BEAM

Éditions Ethos ®
www.editionsethos.com
contact@editionsethos.com

ISBN : 978-84-19006-82-0

Legal deposit : October 25, 2024

Serge Monast (1945-1996) was a Canadian investigative journalist, poet and essayist. He is known to English-speaking readers mainly for Blue Beam Project. He was an active member of the Social Credit Party of Canada. In the early 1990s, he started writing on the theme of the New World Order and conspiracies hatched by secret societies, being particularly inspired by the works of William Guy Carr. He founded the International Free Press Agency (AIPL – Agence Internationale de Presse libre), where he published most of his work on these themes, achieving some prominence with an interview on esotericist and ufologist Richard Glenn's TV show "Ésotérisme Expérimental", in which he repeatedly warned his audience about the dangers of a World Government. In 1994, he published "Le Projet Blue Beam" ("Blue Beam project"), in which he detailed his claim that NASA, with the help of the United Nations, was attempting to implement a New Age religion with the Antichrist at its head and start a New World Order, via a technologically simulated Second Coming of Christ. He also gave talks on this topic. In 1995, he published his most detailed work, "Les Protocoles de Toronto (6.6.6)", modelled upon "The Protocols of the Elders of Zion", wherein he said a Masonic group called "6.6.6" had, for twenty years, been gathering the world's powerful to establish the New World Order and control the minds of individuals. By 1995 and 1996, Monast said he was being hunted by the police and authorities for involvement in "networks of prohibited information". He died of a heart attack in his home in December 1996, at age 51, the day after being arrested and spending a night in jail, under very strange and suspicious conditions.

PUBLISHER'S NOTE

This book is a transcript of a talk given by Serge Monast in 1994 on the subject of NASA's Project Blue Beam. Serge Monast, who claimed to be persecuted by the police and secret services, died two years later, in 1996, in extremely disturbing and dubious circumstances, officially of a "heart attack."

Serge Monast has faithfully exposed the New World Order for the last decade. His children were home-schooled, so the authorities took his eight year old daughter away, then his seven year old son was taken, as they said the parents were abusing them emotionally by stopping the children going to a State school. The father was then arrested, and spent the night in jail. Next day at home, he had a "heart attack." He was 46 years old. This brave man has left a wife, who now has no family.

INTRODUCTION

The infamous NASA [National Aeronautics and Space Administration] Blue Beam Project has four different steps in order to implement the new age religion with the Antichrist at its head. We must remember that the new age religion is the very foundation for the new world government, without which religion the dictatorship of the new world order is completely impossible. I'll repeat that: Without a universal belief in the new age religion, the success of the new world order will be impossible! That is why the Blue Beam Project is so important to them, but has been so well hidden until now.

TRANSCRIPT OF A PRESENTATION GIVEN BY SERGE MONAST ON NASA'S PROJECT BLUE BEAM (1994)

This is the International Free Press in Canada (address given, no longer valid—International Free Press Network, P.O. Box 177, Magog, Quebec, Canada J1X3W8). The International Free Press Network is not a religious group, neither a political organization, but and independent worldwide investigation press agency, in the field of politics, economic, medical and military.

We specialize ourselves in investigating and publishing special reports and audio tapes to expose the under world of the United Nations' conspiracy to implement a New World Order.

Our task is to make the people realize that the coming of the New World Order is not a dream, neither a paranoid thought. It is a real Satanic under going project.

For what?

To abolish all Christian traditional religions in order to replace them by a one-world religion based on the 'cult of man'.

To abolish all national identity and national pride in order to establish a world identity and world pride.

To abolish the family as known today in order to replace it by individuals all working for the glory of one-world government

To destroy all individual artistic and scientific creating works to implement a world government's one mind sight??

And that kind of declaration of war from the United Nations is for:

• the implementation of a universal and obligatory membership to the United Nations, as transcending of the United Nations by multi-military and multi-police force;

• a world wide Justice Department through the United Nations with an International Criminal Court;

• a world wide new Trade Agreement for all nations;

• the end of cold war—of local war like it is today, and the obligation for co-existence for "peace";

• and also, a New World Religion and a New World Culture for all men.

If we really wish to understand the Blue Beam Project —NASA's Blue Beam Project—where is that from?... we have to go back to the dawning of the Age of Aquarius. Remember that song? That song said:

"When the moon is in the seventh house, and Jupiter aligns with mars, and peace will guide our planet, and love will steer the stars."

This related with the year 1982, to be at that time the opening of the conspiracy for the Age of Aquarius. Just before the implementation of the New World Order, supposed to start at that time in 1983… and I have to say that the Blue Beam Project was set up for the year 1983.

It has been delayed at that time. We don't know exactly why, but since 1983, makes eleven years they've really improved themselves with new technology and through space, that enable them right now to make their space show possible.

So, the goals of the New Age movement under which the United Nations operates right now, are the implementation of a New World Messiah.

The tools of the new world government are a multi-national army—an international army; an international police force; a World Bank for the economy; a World Government under the United Nations; a World Conservation Bank for wilderness around the world. That means that all green movements will be melded into this new International Bank or will disappear. A World Religion where all church doctrines will be destroyed at the roots to be replaced by the new religion of the Age of Aquarius.

The world seven rate classifications for all men and women—the new paradise, they said—where everybody will have a predetermined work to fill out whether they agree or not; the world concentration camp headquarters at the United Nations for those who will not accept the new system; the world agriculture and food-supply control which will control food and vitamin supplies all around the world.

The New World Order will be an in-between government system from old USSR, Great Britain and its commonwealths, and the actual United States with its melting-pot population. This is at the end... a new spiritual-political world order which will replace the old one in which we live right now.

What are the New World Order plans? They plan the destruction of all people who believe in the Bible, who worship Jesus Christ, and the complete disappearance of Christianity to achieve this plan.

The New World Order will change nations' laws in order that Christian religious beliefs and symbols—like the cross for instance—will be come unlawful. Only Easter and Christmas for instance will be replaced by New Age festivities around the world.

The New World Order plans also the abolishment of all currencies and the transfer to electronic cash through the super highway—what we call also, the electronic highway. The thinker and the basic doctrine books of the New Age conspiracy for the New World Government are—and listen to the name of those people because all the new way of thinking of the New World Order are from those people, those authors who wrote different kinds of books which are the basic belief of the New Age movement:

Helena Petrovna Blavatsky, who wrote *Isis Unveiled* and *The Secret Doctrine*.

Alice A. Baily who wrote *The Race* and *the Initiation* and the *Externalization of the Hierarchy*. Also, *Initiation,*

Human and Solar; The Reappearance of the Christ—their Christ is the new messiah; *The Destiny of the Nations*, in which they plan what they're going to do with the actual nation-state.

The *Unfinished Autobiography, Discipleship in the New Age, Esoteric Psychology*—that's a writing of Alice Baily, very important for all New Age thinkers who are exactly the ones who plan the New World Order.

Also the writing of Nicholas Roerich wrote Mitreya, that's their new messiah; Shambala the Resplendent; The Agni? Yoga Series.

Also the writing of David Spangler who wrote *Revelation, the Birth of a New Age*, considered as a valuable insight to the New Age movement. *Reflections on the Christ* which is related to the Luciferian initiation; *Links With Space*, which relayed as supposed to be big space show in which aliens are supposed to come to save men. *Relationship and Identity; The Laws of Manifestation;* New Age?, and *Toward a Planetary Vision* which is directly related with the New World Order as they plan it to be.

Now, what do those people also plan?… and as I said before, this is not a dream and this is not paranoid thinking. This is real. So they plan… to accept the New World Order, people will have to accept first the New World Religion. To enter into the New World Religion, the Christians will have to abdicate their own beliefs.

So as they said, especially Benjamin Creme, David Spangler, Alice Baily, Helena Petrovna Blavatsky… all said that the initiation will be on a world basis, inside the new organized Christian church and is a Masonic Lodge, and Order organization. It will be based on a Luciferian initiation, so what we have to understand here is: it won't be possible for somebody who will hold tight to his own Christian beliefs to get into the New World Order. That will be impossible.

Now for those who will not accept the NWO, who will reject it, the new age people—the new ager, the new world order people, which is the same—they plan concentration camps—re-education camps—and for those camps they made what is known to be the rainbow color classification of the new world order prisoner. The rainbow considered as the bridge symbol leading to the Satanic world of the New World Order.

We already do know for instance, that everybody will have to take an oath to Lucifer with a ritual initiation in order to cross that bridge into the new World Order. All resisters to that initiation, as they plan, will definitely be sent to a detention facility where they will be separated in different categories. That's what they call the rainbow color classification of the New World Order prisoner.

Classification of Christian children, as they plan it, are to be used as human sacrifice. Where? Within the black mass ceremonies, they will participate in any kind of sexual orgy, some to be kept as sexual slaves.

Classification 2, which is the classification of prisoners to be used in medical experiments where drugs and new technologies will be tested on humans.

The 3rd classification is the classification of healthy prisoners for the international human organ center, where their vital organs will be removed one by one while they will be be maintained in life with special life-support systems.

Classification 4, for all healthy underground workers. The new world order is a basic worldwide dictatorship based on the Luciferian religion. A dictatorship with the appearance of an international democracy. In order to maintain that democracy illusion, camps and slave labor will be hidden from the populations of the earth. Just remember, for instance, how Hitler covered up the maternity in the concentration camp in his time.

Classification 5, which is the classification of uncertain prisoners in the international re-educational center, where they will be re-educated in order to repent themselves on worldwide t.v. and where they will learn how to glorify the virtues of the new world order for humanity.

Classification 6, which is the international execution center. We're still waiting for details on the 7th rate classification as well as we're still waiting for proof on the color classification for each prisoner section.

Now, those people… this is what they plan in their new paradise world. So you have to understand that when I decided to release—about six months ago—some tiny parts of information concerning their most secret project, which is the NASA Blue Beam project, I was not sure at that time if I would survive my stand against the new world order's most sophisticated project, set up to put down on their knees all men of all nations, cultures and religions.

But now, following my own Christian conscience, my real and deep love for all my unknown brothers and sisters in America and other parts of the world, I fully accept to give my life it that has to be the case, for the truth, for Jesus Christ, by releasing for the first time ever the four major steps of the satellite Blue Beam Project…

What I ask to everyone who will read and hear the description following: It is not to be paralyzed by their natural fear but to spread every word of the contents of this ninety-minute audio tape and to gather together in order to pray, to think and to plan different ways they will organize themselves to survive the New World Order government showdown and power-taking. Because what we have to understand is the New World Government won't be something permanent—immortal. This is not the case. But what we have to do and what we have to think right now is how to organize ourselves to survive such tyranny, such Satanic plans.

Now, the famous NASA Blue Beam Project has four different steps. Four parts toward the implementation of the New World Religion with the anti-Christ at its head. And we must remember that the New World Religion is the basic foundation for the New World Government. Without that New World Religion, such government, such worldwide dictatorship is completely impossible. That's why the project is so not only so important to them, but was so well kept secret to now.

The first step concerns the breakdown of all archeological knowledge. It deals with the set-up of earthquakes at certain precise locations of the planet where supposedly new discoveries will suddenly explain—for them—the wrong meaning of all major religions' basic doctrines. This classification used to make the population believe that all religious doctrines have been misunderstood and misinterpreted have already started with the field of psychological preparation for populations for the first step has been prepared through films like 2001 a Space Odessy; the series, Star Trek; Star Wars which deals with space invasion and space protection; and the last film, Jurassic Park, dealing with the theory of evolution.

Now, which is important to understand in that first step is that those earthquakes will hit at different parts of the world where scientists and archeological teachings have been taught in the past where supposedly there were some hidden secrets. By those kinds of earthquakes it will be possible for them to rediscover again—supposedly, okay?—rediscover again those kinds of secrets and those secrets are meant to discredit all the religions' basic doctrines.

This is the first preparation for the plan for humanity, because what they want to do is to throw down, to shake up the beliefs of all Christians on the planet. And to do that they need some false proof, supposedly from the past, and from the far past that will "prove" to men and women that their religions are false.

The second step deals with the gigantic space show with three dimensional optical holograms and sounds, laser projections of multiple holographic images to different parts of the world, each receiving different images according to predominating regional/national religious faith. This new god's image will be talking in all languages. Now to understand that, we have to go back a little bit in different Secret Services research done in the last 25 years. Like this one:

The Soviets have manufactured the advanced computer, even imported, and fed them with the minute psychical particular base under studies about the anatomy and the biology of the human body; and the studies about the anatomy, the chemistry and the electricity of the human brain. These computers were fed as well, with the different languages and their meanings. The dialect of people have been fed from the Nature Truth satellite. The Soviets started to feed the computer with objective programs like the ones New Messiah. It also seems that the Soviets now, the new world order people, [???...][1] to suicidal methods with the human society by allocating an electronic wave on every mind for many persons in different societies.

Now, there are two different things in that second part. The space show and where that space show comes from. The Space Show, the holographic imaging will be used in a simulation of the ending in which you are given scenes which focus on fulfillment of that which is a desire for you to protect [???...] to fit the needs of those adversary [???...]

The results of this deliberately staged false Christ will be for the implementation of a new universal religion. Enough tricks will be foisted on us to hook us into the lie. The Project is the ability to take up a whole bunch of people as in a rapture type of situation and to whisk the whole bunch into never-never land.

The calculated resistance to the New World Religion, the New World Order and the New Messiah will be [???...] on a massive scale in the ensuing Holy Wars. The Blue Beam Project will pretend to be the universal fulfillment of the prophesies of old, as nature and even as that which took place 2,000 years ago.

In principal, it will make use of the sky as a movie screen, a space based laser generating satellite projects simultaneous images to the four corners of the planet in every language and in every dialect according to region. It

---

1   Not audible (Publisher's note).

deals with the religion aspect of the new world order and is a large scale seduction.

Computers will coordinate the satellite and software will run the show and tell. Holography is based on very nearly identical signal, combining to produce an image or hologram with deep perception which is equally applicable [???...] to ELF, VLF and LF waves. It is an optical phenomena.

Specifically, the show will consist of laser projection of multiple holographic images to different parts of the world, each receiving a different according to predominating regional/national religious faith. Not a single area will be excluded.

With computer animation and sound effects appearing to come from the depths of space, astonished followers of the various creeds will witness their own returned messiah in spectacularly convincing life-like realness. Then the projection of the Christ, of Mohammed, Buddah, Krishna, etc. will merge into one after [???...] explanation of the mysteries, prophecies, and revelation will have been disclosed.

This one god will in fact be the anti-Christ who will explain the various scriptures have been misunderstood, that the religions of all are responsible for turning brother against brother, nation against nation; therefore the world's religions must be abolished to make way for the Golden Age, New Age of the One World Religion, representing the one god anti-Christ in this instance they see before them[1].

---

1   Here are three statements from the *Protocols of the Elders of Zion* :

Naturally this superbly staged [???...] falsification will result in social religious disorder on a grand scale, including millions of programmed religious fanatics, through demonic possession cases on a scale never seen before. In addition, this event will occur at a time of great political anarchy and general tumult at the edge of something big... the United Nations, even though it plans to use the Beethoven song of joy as the official Anthem for the New World Order.

Now, if we put this space show and parallel with the star war program we get this: Combinations of electro-magnetic radiation and hypnosis have also been the subject of intensive research. In 1974, for instance, researcher G. F. Shapis... said of one of these research proposals and this investigation:

> "It will be shown that the spoken word of the hypnotist may also become varied by modulated electro-magnetic energy directly into the [???...] spot of the human brain, without employing any technical device for receiving or transporting the message and without the person exposed to such

"When the hour strikes for our Sovereign Lord of all the World to be crowned it is these same hands [the mob] which will sweep away everything that might be a hindrance thereto." (Protocol No. 3.)
"Ever since that time [French Revolution] we have been leading the peoples from one disenchantment to another, so that in the end they should turn also from us in favour of that King Despot of the blood of Zion, whom we are preparing for the world." (Protocol No. 3.)
"However, it is probably all the same to the world who is its sovereign lord, whether the head of Catholicism or our despot of the blood of Zion." (Protocol No.4.)
(Publisher's note).

influence having a chance to control the information input consciously.

It may be expected that they rationalize their behavior and consider it to be under taken out of their own free will."

Anybody investigating so-called channeling phenomena right now would be wise to take this area of research into consideration. It is interesting to note the fact that the number of people who consider themselves channelers have escalated rapidly since this type of research was conducted.

It is uncanny how similar their messages are regardless of which entity they claim to be the source of their divine guidance. It would suggest that any individual considering the content of channeled information should be discerning and critically evaluate where the message they are receiving or considering it empowering or would serve to invoke thought patterns beneficial to the New World Order.

The Sidney Morning Arrow? Published an item on March 21st, 1983 which asked [???...]. The article states that a paper entitled "The Soviets are Invading the Human Mind" has been submitted to the newspaper foreign editor by Dr. Nathan Ab [???...], Assistant Professor in the [???...] in Egypt. It is worth quoting the article at length even though his grammar is a little old.

This article relates with the subject who manufactured the advanced computer we were talking about a few minutes ago, and which is really important, because these kinds of computers can be around through satellite into space. The computers were fed, as we said as well, with the different languages and their meanings; the dialect of the people has been fed from the Nature Truth satellite.

The Soviets started to feed the computer with objective program. Today, we're not talking about the Soviets, we're talking about the United Nations, the new world order's people. They're the ones who feed the computer right now with objective programs.

Also, the editor of the column in which the article was printed even states, "We think it makes sense too important to ignore." I think that it is considerate way of putting it. One disturbing possibility, given all the information we have at hand, is that the individuals involved in this potential [???...] mind control operation could then sell the program and not even be aware that they are conducting such an operation.

Now, figure it out how far they can go right now.

Now, these techniques push us toward the third step of the NASA Blue Beam project that goes along with the telepathic electronical two-ways communication where ELF, VLF and LF waves will reach the people of the earth by the inside of their brain making each one to believe that his own 'god' is talking to each one from within his own soul.

Such waves from satellite are fed from the memory of computers which store a lot of data about the human being and the languages. These waves will then interlace and interweave with the natural thinking to form what we call [???...] artificial talk. Now that kind of technology goes into the 1970's, 1980's and 1990's research where the human brain has been compared to a computer; information is fed in, processed, integrated and our response is then formulated and acted upon.

Mind controllers manipulate information in the same manner as a computer for grammar manipulates information.

In January, 1991, the University of Arizona hosted a conference titled "The NATO Advanced Research Workshop on Current and Emergent Phenomena in Bio-Molecular Systems".

What does that mean exactly? That means this: If we refer to one paper that was delivered at the conference, stood out for its different attitude toward the development under discussion at that time. It was in effect a protest and a chilling warning to the attending scientists about the potential abuse of their research findings.

Now, what does that paper mean, and state? It states that the United States has [???...] communication equipment which can make the blind see, the deaf hear and the lame walk. It can relieve the terminally ill of all pain without the use of any drugs—and I'm not talking about science fiction over here—a man might retain the use of all his faculties up until the day of his death.

This communication equipment depends on the new way of looking at the human brain and neuro-muscular system and [???...] radiation pulse at ultra low frequency. Some of this equipment is now operational within the Central Intelligence Agency—the CIA—and the Federal Bureau of Investigations. It will never be used to make the blind see and the deaf hear and the lame walk, because it is central to the domestic political agenda and foreign policy of the late president Bush.

Domestically the new communications equipment is being used to torture and murder persons who match profiles imagined; to be able to screen a given population for terrorists; to torture and murder citizens who belong to organizations which promote peace and development in Central America; to torture and murder citizens who belong to organizations opposed to deployment and use of nuclear weapons; and to create a race of slaves called automatons, or what it is popularly called, the Manchurian Candidate.

Over seas experimentation is taking place on [???....] by the United States and Canada, Great Britain, Australia, Germany, Finland and France. In addition there has been a long series of [???....] among British computer scientists of all who have some connection to the United States Navy.

What is possible to ask here in front of such a psychology of terror as this? Would any government, corporation or psychiatrist willfully promote such horror today? The answer is quite obviously, "yes". Government agencies and the corporations that work with them toward New World Order are prepared to promote anything that will help them to achieve their objective of total social control.

As for the question of "why?": for one thing, if you terrify the public and make them fear for their safety they will allow you to implement draconian law enforcement practices, disarm them and keep extensive records on them and they only have to tell you, "Well, that's all in order to protect you, of course".

And secondly, it promotes the decay of the current form of democratic political system and leads societies to search for alternatives to current political methodology.

Of course, the alternative has already been planned. It is called New World Order and it won't have your safety or interest at heart. As George Bush. said, "read my lips."

Fear has always been used by powerful elite to control and subjugate the masses. The old maxim "divide and conquer is being played out to the limit in every corner of the planet to ensure that everybody is frightened for their personal safety and scared or suspicious of those around them. This too, it is called mind control.

Now, to go a little bit further in that new technology which is at the basis of the NASA Blue Beam project, we have to consider this quote from psychologist James V. McConnell, which was published in a 1970 issue of "Psychology Today". He said,

> "The day has come when we can combine sensory deprivation with drugs, hypnosis and astute manipulation of reward and punishment to gain almost absolute control over an individual's behavior.

> It should be then possible to achieve a very rapid and highly effective type of positive brainwashing that would allow us to make dramatic change in a person's behavior and personality."

Now when we talked before about that kind of rays and the telepathic electronic two-ways communication... the kinds of rays which are fed from the memory of computers which store a lot of data about the human being and the languages; and we said that the people of the earth will be reached by the inside of their brain making each one to believe that his own 'god' is talking to each one within his own soul, we refer to that kind of technology and that kind of thinking.

That same psychologist said,

"We should reshape society so that we all would be trained from birth to want to do what societies want us to do. We have the techniques to do it. No one owns his own personality."

And this quote here is real important because it is also basic teaching from the United Nations, that 'no one owns his own personality'. The same psychologist adds:

"You have no say about what kind of personality you acquire, and there's no reason to believe you should have the right to refuse to acquire a new personality if your old one is anti-social."

Which is important in that kind of declaration here, if the NWO will be set up over the old one, that means that the old way of thinking, the way we think right now—our behavior, our religious beliefs—would be considered by those people as old thinking, an old way of living, and they will have—to change it—the re-education camps of the United Nations, to make sure that people will have—for them an anti-social behavior which is today an actual one— will be re-educated in a way to have the new behavior to fulfill the needs of the NWO.

Might it be the largest mind control project ever? because NASA Blue Beam Project is also for the implementation of a New World Religion, a mind control project. So I would suggest you examine the evidence carefully before you disregard this possibility.

Now, if we go further in the different reports we have over here, we find this: The mind control operation and technology include a transmitter which broadcasts at the frequency of the human nervous system, which system is manufactured by the Laurel Electro-Optical System in Pasadena, California.

Laurel, a major defense contractor had previously conducted research on directed-energy weapons for Lieutenant-General Leonard Perez of the U.S. Air Force who was searching for a weapon to implant messages into the minds of the enemy and to urge his own truth onto superhuman deeds of valor.

The device employs electro-magnetic radiation of jigars? frequency pulse at extremely low frequency—ELF. It is used to torture people both physically and mentally from a distance.

Weapons of this type are claimed to have been used against a British woman protesting the presence of American cruise missiles at Greensam? Common Air Base during the '70s.

This weapon can be used to induce total sensory deprivation by broadcasting signals into the auditory nerves at such a power that it blocks the victims ability to 'hear themselves think'. The device has taken the concept of the old phrase "It is so noisy in here I can't hear myself think", and turned it into a powerful weapon of terror.

The process employed by such ELF technologies are described in various U.S. Defense Department Publications, including one entitled, *The Electro-Magnetic Spectrum and Low Intensity Conflict*, by Captain Paul E. Tyler, medical [???...], United States Navy, which is included in a collection entitled, *Low Intensity Conflicts in Modern Technology* edit by Lt. Colonel, David [???...] U.S. Air Force. The paper was delivered in 1984, and the collection published in 1986 by Air University Press, Maxwell Air Force Base, Alabama.

"Another pulse microwave device can deliver audible signals directly to an individual while they remain undetectable by anyone else. The technology is very simple, and can be built using an ordinary police radar gun. The microwave beam generated by the device is moderated at audio frequencies and can broadcast voices directly into the brain."

...and here we come for that NASA Blue Beam Project, as we were talking about at the beginning, the telepathic electronic two-way communications from space goes exactly with that kind of technology.

I repeat here,

"the microwave beam generated by the device is modulated at audio frequencies and can broadcast voices directly into the brain".

In his book, The Body Electric, Nobel Prize nominee Robert Becker described a series of experiments conducted in the early 1960's by Olenfree, where this phenomena was first demonstrated as well as later experiment [???...] in 1973 at the Walter Reed Army Institute of Research by Dr. Joseph C. Sharp, who personally underwent tests in which he proved he could hear and understand spoken words delivered to him in an echo-free isolation chamber via a pulse microwave audiogram, an analogue of the word sound vibration beamed into his brain.

Becker then goes on to state,

"such a device has obvious application and covert operation designed to drive a target crazy with voice or deliver undetectable instruction to a programmed asset".

Now figure out, when we talked about that new messiah from space would be talking to different religious and faith people on the earth by the inside who would give such kind of instruction like to Muslim people what kind of possession case and kind of social disorder on a large case scale ever seen before we would see everywhere on the planet.

A 1978 book entitled *Microwave auditory effects and applications*, by James C. Lim, explains how audible voice can be broadcast directly into the brain. This technology could be used to make the deaf hear, but instead it has been turned against the public.

Olenfree also reported that he could speed up, slow down or stop isolated frogs hearts by synchronizing the pulse rate of a microwave beat with the beat of the earth itself. According to Robert Becker, similar results have been obtained using live frogs, indicating that it is technically feasible to produce heart attacks which are rays designed to penetrate the human chest.

I should mention also that Becker does not participate in such research. It has been demonstrated that focused Ultra High Frequency—UHF—electromagnetic energy beams can be used to induce considerable agitation and muscular or induce muscular weakness and lethargy. Microwaves can also be used to burn human skin, and aide the effect of drugs, bacteria and poisons, or effect the functioning of the entire brain.

These effects were all studied at length by the CIA on September 21, 1977 in testimony before the Senate Sub-committee on Health and Scientific Research. Dr. Sidney Gottlieb who directed the MK Ultra program at that time was forced to discuss aspects of the CIA's research to find technique of vacuation, the human organs, by remote electronic means.

So this is something that exists right now, that has been pushed to its highest degree and that can be used from space by satellite to reach anybody on the planet.

If we go a little bit deeper in that kind of process and mind control over the people, we find for the year 1988 this: the equipment and technology... that kind of technology of mind control have been used to influence politics in a much more direct fashion.

Michael Dukakis, the Democrat Presidential candidate running against George Bush in the 1988 U.S. election, was targeted with microwave technology in order to impede his public speaking performance when the opinion polls he posed a threat to Bush's election prospect. He also claims that the equipment was used against Kitty Dukakis and drove her to the brink of suicide. In the grisly Disneyland World of U.S. politics a presidential candidate with problems such as these two dealt with, obviously stand to lose the race to the White House.

What I can add over here about those kinds of new mental battlefields that will be used in the NASA Blue Beam Project to implement the New World Religion is this: In the December 1980 edition of the U.S. Army Journal, which is called *Military Review*, an article by Lieutenant Colonel John B. Alexander, entitled *The New Mental Battlefield: Beam Me Up, Spock*, provides further insight into the technical capabilities now at the disposal of the controllers. He writes:

"Several examples will demonstrate areas in which progress has been made:

The transference of energy from one organism to another.

The ability to heal or cause disease can be transmitted over a distance, thus inducing illness or death for no apparent cause.

Telepathic behavior modification which includes the ability to induce hypnotic states up to distances in excess of 1,000 kilometers has been reported. The use of telepathic hypnosis also holds great potential. This capability could allow agents to be deeply planted with no conscious knowledge of their programming, and [???...] the Manchurian Candidate [???...] and does not even require a phone call.

Other mind to mind induction techniques are being considered. If perfected, this capability could allow the direct transference of thought via telepathy from one mind or group of minds to a select target audience. The unique factor is that the recipient will not aware that thought has been implanted from an external source. He or she will believe the thoughts are original".

This is exactly what we were talking about, and the third step of the NASA Blue Beam Project calls the telepathic-electronic two-way communication, and the article continues:

"If it is possible to feed artificial thoughts into the [???...] genetic [???...] via satellite the mind control of the entire planet is now possible. An individual's only resistance to constantly question the motivation behind their thoughts and not act upon thoughts that they consider to be outside the boundaries of their own ethical and moral boundaries."

Once again, it is wise to consider how television, advertising and various forms of social pressure are constantly being used to manipulate those boundaries.

And one thing... another thing which is really important over here, dealing with that kind of technology is this: It has been reported by Lt. Col. Alexander who said in the summary of his Military Review article:

"The information on those kinds of technology presented here would be considered by some to be ridiculous since it does not conform to their view of reality; but some people still believe the world is flat."

Now, this means a lot, because if people do not believe that kind of technology to be possible, or this kind of technology we're talking about is just science fiction... those people put themselves in jeopardy because when the night of the thousand stars will shine from the space during that night when the new messiah and the new world religion will be implemented on the planet, those people won't have time to prepare themselves, and they will not be prepared to preserve themselves against such kind of technology.

That's why they put themselves in jeopardy. Because they don't believe; they don't take time to prepare and this is something real dangerous. Now we're going to talk about the fourth step of that NASA Blue Beam project. Now, the fourth step concerns the universal supernatural manifestation with electronic means. It contains three different orientations.

One is to make mankind belief that an alien invasion is about to strike down on each major city of the earth in order to push each major nations to use its nuclear to strike back. This way, it would put each of these nations in a state of full disarmament in front of the United Nations after the false attack.

The second is to make the Christians believe to a major rapture with the supposedly divine intervention of an alleged good alien force coming to save the people from a brutal satanic attack. Its goal is to get rid of all significant opposition to the New World Order.

The third orientation in the fourth step is a mixture of electronic and supernatural forces. The waves used at that time will allow supernatural forces to travel through optical fiber, coaxial cable… the one used for cable TV, electric and phone lines in order to penetrate everywhere on electronic equipment, appliances will be already installed with microchips. The goal of this one deals with global Satanic ghosts—spector—all around the world in order to push all population on the edge to drown into a wave of suicide, killing and permanent psychological disorders.

Then after that night of the thousand stars humanity is going to be ready to implore any new messiah to re-establish peace everywhere at any cost, even at the cost of freedom abdication. Now which is interesting to note this over here: the technique used in that fourth step is exactly the same used in the past in USSR to force the people to accept Communism. The same technical wave will be used by the United nations to implement the New World Religion in the New World Order.

A lot of people ask me when this is going to happen and how they are going to do it. Which are the steps they're going to set up before that Night of the Thousand Stars? According to different research and different reports that we get, they are thinking right now of an economic crash. Not a complete crash that would put down all the economy, but an economic crash that would force them… that will also have them as a pretext to come up with an in between currency.

That means a new kind of currency that would be in between the currency that we have right now and the electronic cash. Now, what they want to do with the in between currency is to force everybody who has some money in reserve everywhere to spend that money, because they consider that they will have problems to implement the New World Order if somewhere there are some people independent who can survive by themselves, so they have to put the people in a way to force them to spend everything and absolutely everything they have.

That's why they want to start with a kind of organized economic crash to put up a new currency, and after that, they're planning to put on worldwide basis the electronic cash. But right now it is not possible for them to put that electronic cash since the super highway—what we call also the electronic highway—is not yet ready and implemented all over the planet.

To implement the electronic cash worldwide they have to have finished the implementation of the super highway everywhere, and for people wondering what the super highway is exactly... the super highway is an electronic sophisticated way to control directly the people in every home where it will be implemented or installed. To that stage, the control—the political control—of everybody on the planet will be possible.

To prevent any kind of independence from the people we have to remember that the New Agers... the New World Order people will do anything to make sure that everybody, before the year 2000 will have spent all his personal and reserve cash or goods.

To prevent also any kind of independence the New World people have already started, all over the planet, to put into birds, fish and wild animals microchip implants. Why? Because they want to make sure that for the people who won't accept the NWO, they won't be able to fish or hunt anywhere, because the day they would try in the wilderness to make some fishing and hunting, the day they would catch a fish or an animal with a microchip implant they would be traceable by satellite, absolutely, everywhere.

Those same people to make sure of full control of everybody are changing laws of different countries right now to make sure they will have full control of the vitamins. They are also changing laws right now about religion, and also about psychiatric disorders, in order to consider anybody with a violence potential as somebody who has psychiatric disorder and has to be put in a clinic to be re-educated.

If you keep in mind that this New World Order New World Government is a worldwide dictatorship you cannot forget that a dictatorship will do everything possible to make sure they will be in a position to control anybody everywhere on the planet. That's why the kind of new technology they're putting on right now everywhere is a technology for control of the people.

If you take, for instance, the technology that we had in the 1940s and the 1950s that kind of technology was made to help the people for an easier life. But the new technology —if you take the time to look at computers, microchips, new microchip cars, super highway… you'll notice, and this is evident, you'll notice that all that technology is built in a way to track down and control anybody everywhere. And as that kind of technology is made in such a way, it's made also for a purpose.

To refuse to see that purpose is not to want to see the evidence of a new kind of political power that want to establish themselves all over the planet.

Now, at the end of this conference… I want to apologize to every-bodies my difficulties, my problem with English speaking, because as a Canadian journalist I'm also from the eastern part of Canada which is French-speaking country.

I hope that even if I have problems with pronunciation, or a French accent in my speaking, I hope it will be possible for everybody at least to understand the meaning of this conference and also the real meaning of the NASA Blue Beam Project.

And I ask everybody everywhere who will be listening that they make everything possible to spread the words everywhere about that kind of new technology which exists right now into space and which exists for the purpose to implement the New World Religion which is also the basic foundation of the New World Order government.

Thank you and good night.

TABLE OF CONTENTS

ETHOS

Éditions Ethos ®
www.editionsethos.com
contact@editionsethos.com